Total Abandonment

TO GOD'S WILL

SCIENCE
of
SAINTHOOD

SCIENCE *of* SAINTHOOD

Nihil Obstat
The Reverend James M. Dunfee, MA, STL
Censor Librorum
March 9, 2025

Imprimatur
The Most Reverend Edward M. Lohse, JCD
Apostolic Administrator of Steubenville
March 11, 2025

The *nihil obstat* and *imprimatur* do not signify agreement with the content, opinions, or statements expressed but simply affirm that the content does not contradict faith and morals.

Scripture verses are from The Revised Standard Version of the Bible: Catholic Edition, copyright © 1965, 1966 the Division of Christian Education of the National Council of the Churches of Christ in the United States of America. Used by permission. All rights reserved.

Video Study Written by Matthew Leonard

Workbook Written by Matthew Leonard & John Paul Nunez

Cover Design and layout by Patty Borgman

Science Of Sainthood | ScienceOfSainthood.com

Table of Contents

Welcome to the Science of Sainthood

Welcome to *Total Abandonment to God's Will*, presented by the Science of Sainthood.

Founded by evangelist Matthew Leonard, the Science of Sainthood is one of the world's premier online Catholic communities dedicated to teaching authentic Catholic spirituality. Steeped in the tradition of Saints like John of the Cross, Teresa of Avila, and Thomas Aquinas, our goal is to guide regular Catholics, step by step, down the path to nothing less than sainthood.

More than education, this is *transformation*!

How to Use This Workbook

This study is just one of many powerful courses on Catholic spirituality you'll find at ScienceOfSainthood.com. Visit the site to learn more.

Each lesson in this study contains the following sections:

- Short Introduction
- Review of the Previous Lesson
- Lesson Video
- Space to Take Notes on the Video Lesson
- A Passage from a Saint

- A Passage from Sacred Scripture for Lectio Divina
- Written Meditation
- Review & Discussion Questions
- Prayer Journal

How you use the sections depends completely on what works best for you and/or your group. The written sections are there for either group or individual use. Some groups simply discuss the video and leave the journaling and other content for use outside the gathering. Other groups work their way through each portion together, reading the passages aloud. Again, it's entirely up to your discretion.

As you can see, we have provided Review and Discussion Questions to help spur group discussion.

Each video is roughly twelve to fifteen minutes long. This means it would be quite easy to do two lessons in one group study session. That said, the material is designed for flexibility. Use it in the manner most fitting for your group.

Finally, don't forget this study is just one of many within the Science of Sainthood.

If you would like information on an individual subscription or want to find out about parish or group memberships, visit **ScienceOfSainthood.com**!

In a Group Study But Want to Watch on Your Own, Too?

Enjoy the course on your own time with a great discount on a One Year rental of *Total Abandonment to God's Will*.

It's the perfect way to get as much as possible out of this study!

Scan the QR Code with your Phone's Camera & Tap the Link!

LESSON ONE

Beginning Our Sweet Surrender

Lesson Introduction

Abandonment to the will of God is the goal of the Christian life. And yet, surrendering everything over to God remains very difficult for the vast majority of us. What we need to realize is that while giving ourselves over to the Lord's perfect will is absolutely necessary, it's a gradual, step by step process of growth.

 **NOW BEGIN THE VIDEO**

Notes

What The Saints Say

"Perfection is founded entirely on the love of God: 'Charity is the bond of perfection;' and perfect love of God means the complete union of our will with God's."

SAINT ALPHONSUS LIGUORI — *18th Century Doctor of the Church & Founder of the Redemptorists*

Lectio Divina

"Not every one who says to me, 'Lord, Lord,' shall enter the kingdom of heaven, but he who does the will of my Father who is in heaven. On that day many will say to me, 'Lord, Lord, did we not prophesy in your name, and cast out demons in your name, and do many mighty works in your name?'

And then will I declare to them, 'I never knew you; depart from me, you evildoers.'"

MATTHEW 7:21–23

Meditation

While we have a tendency to view abandonment to the will of God as a kind of "next step" in the Christian life, the reality is quite different. Rather than a second or third "phase", it's the beginning, middle, and end of our walk with God.

Jesus is quite clear. If we do not do the will of God, he will forbid us entry into the kingdom of heaven. We will be cast into hell.

And notice that Christ says that even those who prophesied in his name and performed miracles will be cast into the eternal fire (Matthew 7). In other words, we can't simply look at the "success" of our (or other's) various spiritual endeavors like teaching or works of mercy, and think this assures salvation. Don't forget that the bad king Saul prophesied (1 Samuel 10). Pharaoh's demonic priests performed miracles (Exodus 7). Even the traitor Judas Iscariot likely brought people into the faith.

Spiritual success is not defined by signs, wonders or number of converts.

The only way we can be confident to the degree possible of eternal *life* with God is to conform ourselves to the eternal *will* of God. This is not an "extra" to the Christian life. It is the only path.

And while there may be times when we're afraid of what may come our way when we abandon ourselves to the Lord's will, don't forget that he has already walked the same path before us. He has already paved the path with divine grace so that we can follow him without fear.

Review Questions

1. What was Jesus' great act of self-surrender that serves as a model for us to imitate in every aspect of our lives? How does Our Lady imitate this self-surrender in the Annunciation story?

2. What is the highest virtue, the very goal of the spiritual life? Why is this the end goal?

3. What does surrender in every aspect of our lives ultimately lead to? In other words, what necessarily follows if we make a gift of our life like Christ?

4. What does Jesus mean when he says "Be perfect, as your heavenly Father is perfect"?

5. What does St. John say drives out all fear?

Discussion Questions

1. One of the biggest things that keeps us from fully giving ourselves over to the Lord is fear. In particular, we fear that God isn't going to take care of us. What are some particular fears that hold you back from fully surrendering to the Lord and trusting in his loving care for you?

2. Despite what we often like to think, the truth is that we're not in control of our lives. Only God is. But we often forget this, and instead we try to play puppet master over the almost infinite number of situations we face each day.

What are some ways that you've tried to control things over which you actually had no control at all? Do things always work out the way you want when you attempt to exert control? Can you think of situations in which you did not attempt to manipulate the situation? How did they turn out?

Prayer Journal

LESSON TWO

How Can God Participate in Evil?

What We Covered in Our Last Lesson

Right before Jesus died, he cried out, "Father, into thy hands I commit my spirit" (Luke 23:46). Despite being abused, beaten, and seemingly abandoned by God, he still abandoned himself to God. As Catholics, we are supposed to imitate this act of self-surrender in every aspect of our lives. That's the focus of this entire course.

In fact, there's a sense in which everything in the spiritual life leads to this—the abandonment of our will, the abandonment of our lives—into the hands of God. And when we put it into practice, we will find that it's the ultimate key to deep peace, security, and incredible joy both now and forever.

To that end, we're going to learn how to take the events and circumstances of this life and not allow them to upset us or destroy our peace. And we can do this because we're giving ourselves over to a God who loves us desperately; a God who calls us his son or daughter; a God who has not only already walked this path, but literally gave himself for us so that we can follow in his footsteps.

And when you think about it, this gift of self is really at the heart of abandoning oneself to God. Self-giving love is the highest of the virtues. It's the goal of the spiritual life because it's the very life of God.

Admittedly, that may sound scary. If it does, that simply means you're human. Even Christ was scared in his humanity as he sweated blood at Gethsemane. Learning to trust God and abandon ourselves to him doesn't happen overnight. Rather, this is a gradual process of healing the wounds left over from the Original Sin of our first parents, Adam and Eve.

In fact, what we're going to see is that there are stages of abandonment that fit "hand in glove" with the basic stages of the spiritual life we've discussed in other courses in the Science of Sainthood. It's all connected.

Of course, this process of growth and surrender takes some understanding and some work. After all, if we're going to conform our will to God's, we have to be able to discern God's will in the first place. We also have to become aware of the lurking spiritual dangers with which the Devil has successfully deluded many a Catholic.

All of that said, let's not forget that God is our loving Father. And perfect love, says St. John, drives out all fear (1 John 4:18).

Lesson Introduction

If we're going to abandon ourselves totally to God, we need to fully believe that he is in control of everything. But if that's the case, how do we reconcile the existence of terrible evil in the world with an all-loving, all-good, all-holy God?

 **NOW BEGIN THE VIDEO**

Notes

What the Saints Say

"The highest perfection consists not in interior favors or in great raptures or in visions or in the spirit of prophecy, but in the bringing of our wills so closely into conformity with the will of God that, as soon as we realize he wills anything, we desire it ourselves with all our might, and take the bitter with the sweet, knowing that to be His Majesty's will."

ST. TERESA OF AVILA — *16th Century Spanish mystic & Doctor of the Church*

Lectio Divina

"You have heard that it was said, 'You shall love your neighbor and hate your enemy.' But I say to you, Love your enemies and pray for those who persecute you, so that you may be sons of your Father who is in heaven; for he makes his sun rise on the evil and on the good, and sends rain on the just and on the unjust."

MATTHEW 5:43–45

Meditation

Conforming our will to that of God cannot be separated from the commands of God. In other words, aligning our lives with God starts with what we already know he wants us to do. Namely, keep the commandments.

And chief among these commandments is love... even love of our enemies.

Unfortunately, many Christians think it's enough to not hate those against us. But that's not what Christ says. "For if you love those who love you, what reward have you? Do not even the tax collectors do the same" (Matthew 5:46)?

And while it might seem like too high of a bar to actually love those who wound or persecute us, St. Jerome says that's because we're looking at it the wrong way.

"Many measuring the commandments of God by their own weakness, not by the strength of the saints, hold these commands for impossible, and say that it is virtue enough not to hate our enemies, but to love them is a command beyond human nature to obey. But it must be understood that Christ enjoins not impossibilities but perfection. Such was the temper of David towards Saul and Absalom; the Martyr Stephen also prayed for his enemies while they stoned him, and Paul wished himself anathema for the sake of his persecutors."[1]

In other words, we can do it, but we need Christ. We need to grow in perfection so that we can become such a powerful vessel of love that we "naturally" love our enemies and echo Our Lord as he gazed at his own persecutors saying, "Father, forgive them; they know not what they do" (Luke 23:34).

[1] Thomas Aquinas. (1841). Catena Aurea: Commentary on the Four Gospels, Collected out of the Works of the Fathers; St. Matthew (J. H. Newman, Ed.; Vol. 1, p. 206). John Henry Parker.

Review Questions

1. What are the three stages of our growth in abandonment to God?

2. Does God ever create evil?

3. Since nothing happens outside of God's will, does this mean he is ever the cause of evil? Can you explain why?

4. What are the two kinds of evil? What are some examples of each?

5. How does existing outside of time allow God to bring good out of evil?

Discussion Questions

1. Even though God works everything for our good, it's not always easy to see how. Sometimes, we simply don't know how certain events fit into his perfect plan for us, and in those moments, we just have to trust that he knows what he's doing.

What are some times in your life when you've had to abandon yourself to God and trust him in this way? Did you ever find out later how he used any suffering or evil you witnessed to bring about good?

2. Forgiveness is hard, particularly when it comes to those who have wounded us or caused us harm in some way. Think carefully. Are there people in your life that you still have not forgiven? Does seeing these people as instruments God is using to perfect us change your view of them and the harm they caused you? Looking back, can you see how God used any difficult relationships and situations to strengthen your faith and smooth out your spiritual rough edges?

Prayer Journal

LESSON THREE

Overcoming Fear of Abandonment

What We Covered in Our Last Lesson

Just as we grow up in the natural life, so too are there stages of growth in the *super*natural life. And this same principle applies to our ability to abandon ourselves to God's will. There are three different stages of growth in our process of surrender, or abandonment to God. We move from accepting God's will, to obeying his will, to being his instrument. And we're going to loosely follow this structure as we move forward.

But first, we have to acknowledge the fact that God is in control of everything. If we're going to abandon ourselves to him, we need to first fully accept that nothing happens outside of his will. Nothing happens that he doesn't control in some way.

And when we say that God is in control of all things, we mean all things, the good and the bad. But if God is all-good, how can his will be done even when evil is being committed? To answer that, we need to make some distinctions. First of all, God is all pure and all holy, so he is never the cause of sin. Even so, because God is the creator of time and exists both inside and outside of it, he already knows what sin is going to occur. Because of this, he can use every different circumstance for our good.

Secondly, we have to distinguish between two kinds of evil: physical and moral. Physical evil is suffering or pain that isn't directly caused by an immoral act. Rather, it's something that happens according to the laws of nature, but results in suffering because we live in a fallen world. Moral evil is a completely different animal. It occurs when someone willfully acts against the good. It's the result of willful sin or negligence.

Because God is the creator of the universe and nothing can happen without him sustaining it, there's a sense in which he participates in everything. Even so, he cannot be the cause of evil. He can, however, bring good out of it.

And this understanding leads to a whole new view of forgiveness of those who have wronged us. If we can get to the point where we can recognize and accept that everything that happens to us—good and bad—is from God, we can begin to see people who harm us as instruments that God is using to perfect us. And the more we realize this, the easier it becomes to "love your enemy" as Christ commanded.

Lesson Introduction

When it comes to total abandonment to God's will, the "elephant in the room" is always suffering. None of us naturally wants to endure hardship. For this reason, the very idea of surrendering ourselves to God often leads to fear of abandonment. But once we understand more of what the Lord is asking, the fear begins to melt away.

 **NOW BEGIN THE VIDEO**

Notes

What the Saints Say

"It is You Jesus, stretched out on the cross, who gives me strength and are always close to the suffering soul. Creatures will abandon a person in his suffering, but You, O Lord, are faithful."

ST. FAUSTINA KOWALSKA — *20th Century Polish nun & mystic who inspired devotion to the Divine Mercy*

Lectio Divina

"Now great multitudes accompanied him; and he turned and said to them, 'If any one comes to me and does not hate his own father and mother and wife and children and brothers and sisters, yes, and even his own life, he cannot be my disciple. Whoever does not bear his own cross and come after me, cannot be my disciple.'"

LUKE 14:25–27

Meditation

When Christ speaks of us picking up our cross and following him, he's not simply talking about specific sufferings that we're called to endure. Certainly that's part of it, but at its root is an attitude of self-sacrifice that's meant to help us become *like* Christ.

Sacrifice on its own is just that—sacrifice. It hurts. And we all know that something can be painful without changing us.

This was obviously the case for many of the Israelites. After sinning at the foot of Mount Sinai by worshiping the infamous Golden Calf, they had to offer a penitential daily sacrifice. But many did it grudgingly. It was simply a requirement they fulfilled so as to abide by God's decree.

But that's not what God wanted from them. And it's not what he wants from us, either.

The sacrifices we make, the crosses he gives us to bear, are meant to change our hearts. "For I desire steadfast love and not sacrifice, the knowledge of God, rather than burnt offerings," declares Hosea 6:6.

God's goal is always sacrificial love. The crosses he gives us are opportunities to manifest that love. They are opportunities for trustful surrender. They're purposeful. Borne with fortitude and trust, they're not meant to weigh us down. Rather, when accepted with trust, they reshape us into the image of the Christ. Not just the crucified Christ, but the glorified and resurrected Christ. In other words, joined to that of Jesus, it is our crosses that lead us to eternal life.

Review Questions

1. What event was the culmination of Jesus' life of self-surrender?

2. Since we can't totally surrender on our own, what do we need from God in order to begin to give everything over to him?

3. What does Jesus mean when he tells us to pick up our cross and follow him? Is he asking us to do exactly what he has done or is it something more personal?

4. What do our crosses consist of most of the time?

5. Does God ever ask of us something we can't do? Why or why not?

Discussion Questions

1. While we often like to think of our crosses as major challenges that require heroic sacrifice, that's not always the case. What are some little, mundane crosses that you have to endure as part of your daily life? Does seeing them as a path to eternal life change the way you view them?

2. St. Peter thought he was ready to totally abandon himself to the Lord in Gethsemane, but he learned the hard way that he didn't have that kind of spiritual strength yet. Have you ever thought you were ready to surrender more of yourself only to fall short? How did you handle your weakness? Did God use those moments to teach you to humbly trust in his grace and gradual guidance instead of your own strength?

Prayer Journal

LESSON FOUR

The Duty of the Present Moment

What We Covered in Our Last Lesson

We dread suffering. After all, as weak humans, how can we look forward to a life joined to the Cross of Christ? How can we even think it's possible? Well, in order to get past our human frailties on this, there are two main points to keep in mind. First, there's no reason to really be afraid because Christ is totally gentle with us and helps us grow gradually in surrender.

Remember, even the abandonment of Christ at Calvary was the culmination of a life spent in self-surrender. Yes, Jesus was always in total union with the Father and able to surrender himself completely at any given moment. His entire life was self-surrender. But there's a sense in which his life on earth showed us the growth process that we're to undergo as we make our way toward union with the Father, as well. We're following his lead.

And like everything else, this begins with grace. Abandonment to God is not something you just decide to do and "bingo", you're there. Yes, it's an act of the will. But our initial decision, our first "yes" to God can only happen through God.

Secondly, we need to understand what Christ meant when he said, "If any man would come after me, let him deny himself and take up his cross and follow me" (Matthew 16:24). He doesn't mean *his* cross, so to speak; he means our *own* cross, our personal cross. Each of us is a unique person, and while the overall trajectory of our spiritual lives is going to be similar, how it plays out in our individual lives is going to look different. So the crosses he gives us are unique.

And most of the time they're not some giant, looming issue in our life. Certainly there are major challenges that present themselves to us at any given point in time. In fact, we may carry a large cross throughout our entire life. But even when that's the case, the bulk of our personal cross is made up of the splinters of daily life. In other words, our Father isn't marching us up Golgotha right from the get-go.

What's more, Jesus always carries the bulk of the load. Like Simon of Cyrene, we're in a totally supporting role, even when we fully abandon ourselves. But there's a real sense in which we don't even do that. Because at the end of the day, it's all

Christ. Our abandonment can only happen because he gives us the grace to make it happen.

And in the end, the purpose of all this is our eternal salvation. When we pick up our cross and follow Jesus, we take the sorrows we're going to experience anyway because of human sin, and transform them into a means of sanctifying our souls. Simply put, we climb our cross to heaven.

Lesson Introduction

While we have a tendency to view abandonment to God's will as something that we're moving toward, the reality is that our surrender primarily takes place in the present moment. And fully understanding this fundamental truth radically transforms our ability to remain at peace no matter the circumstances in which we find ourselves.

 **NOW BEGIN THE VIDEO**

Notes

What the Saints Say

"As to the past, let us entrust it to God's mercy, the future to divine Providence. Our task is to live holy the present moment."

ST. GIANNA MOLLA — *20th Century Italian pediatrician who died from complications resulting from her refusal to terminate the pregnancy of her fourth child. She is the patron saint of all mothers.*

Lectio Divina

"Therefore do not be anxious, saying, 'What shall we eat?' or 'What shall we drink?' or 'What shall we wear?' For the Gentiles seek all these things; and your heavenly Father knows that you need them all. But seek first his kingdom and his righteousness, and all these things shall be yours as well.

Therefore do not be anxious about tomorrow, for tomorrow will be anxious for itself. Let the day's own trouble be sufficient for the day."

MATTHEW 6:31–34

Meditation

The above passage from Matthew is certainly one of the classic texts with regard to God's providential care of his children. It's an exhortation for us to live in the present moment because God knows our temporal needs and exactly when to provide for them.

"That Physician to whom we have entirely entrusted ourselves," says St. Augustine, "knows when He will give and when He will withhold, as He judges most for our advantage. So that should these things ever be lacking to us, (as God to exercise us often permits,) it will not weaken our fixed purpose, but rather confirm it when wavering."[1]

In other words, God knows exactly what he's doing with us and his timing is always perfect.

But there's a bigger picture here, as well. And it can be seen in other translations of verse 33. For example, in the Douay-Rheims translation, the verse is rendered, "Seek ye therefore first the kingdom of God, and his justice, and all these things shall be added unto you."

The bigger picture is the fact that Christ seems to be referencing something beyond our temporal needs. Yes, he will feed us better than the "birds of the air" and clothe us more beautifully than the "lilies of the field" (Matthew 6:26, 27).

But he's also promising that what is to come is going to be better than what we now have.

As St. John Chrysostom comments, "And He said not, Shall be given, but, Shall be added, that you may learn that the things that are now, are nought to the greatness of the things that shall be."[2]

Put simply, one of the main reasons we shouldn't be anxious is that the lacking we experience in this life is completely temporary. One way or the other, the cares of this world are going to pass away. And as long as we continue to put them into the hands of God and not let them trouble our spirit, God will eventually lead us into an eternal bliss so incredible that all memory of any lacking we experience in this life will be completely erased.

[1] Thomas Aquinas. (1841). *Catena Aurea: Commentary on the Four Gospels, Collected out of the Works of the Fathers: St. Matthew* (J. H. Newman, Ed.; Vol. 1, p. 261). John Henry Parker.

[2] Ibid

Review Questions

1. Is abandonment to God primarily about the past, the present, or the future? Why?

2. What is the only way to adequately prepare to abandon ourselves to God in the big issues that may arise in our lives?

3. Who does the path of perfection lead us to put first? How does it lead us to view ourselves?

4. The duty of the present moment essentially boils down to one virtue. Which virtue is it?

Discussion Questions

1. The duty of the present moment isn't just about the duties associated with our station in life. It also involves our response to things we can't control, like the weather. Can you think of any times when you've had to abandon yourself to God's will in a situation that was entirely out of your control? How did you respond? Would you try to respond differently now?

2. Situations that impact us negatively can often be blessings for someone else. For example, a heavy downpour that impinges on our travel plans might be desperately needed by a farmer. A delayed flight may mean someone else makes it on to the plane. Can you think of any specific situations that were bad for you but sorely needed blessings for someone else? Can you think of any situations in which you were the recipient of something good that "negatively" affected someone else?

Prayer Journal

LESSON FIVE

When Abandonment Gets Messy

What We Covered in Our Last Lesson

While the duty of the present moment may sound simple, actually embracing this concept isn't as easy as it seems. We have a tendency to think "big picture" all of the time, and our gaze is mostly pointed to the future. On one level, that's natural because we're ultimately thinking about our salvation. But there's a big danger in this tendency that can totally derail our ascent to God.

Namely, we might forget that abandonment isn't just a future thing. In fact, it's not even *primarily* a future thing. It's primarily a "present moment" thing. Why? Because the past is behind us, and the future is the "not yet." The only place in which we can actually abandon ourselves is the moment in which we find ourselves right now.

However, we often don't really like to live in the real world, the right now. Most of our lives aren't particularly exciting. They're mundane. But the reality is that our abandonment lies in all the mundanities and annoyances of everyday life, like that stack of dirty dishes or the lawn that needs to be mowed.

In fact, our conformity to God in these ordinary annoyances is the only way we can adequately prepare ourselves for the bigger issues that may arise. If we can't abandon ourself when a fly is buzzing around our head, we're never going to be able to abandon ourself when a big issue presents itself.

In practical terms, this kind of abandonment embraces the fact that God's will is present in this very moment and that to the best of our ability we should react to our circumstances in the manner that God wishes. And we're not only talking about duties associated with our particular vocation. We're also talking about situations we can't control, like the weather.

When we accept God's will like this, it leads us out of ourselves. It leads us to put God and others first. This is a big point. We often forget that the plight of others is a huge part of this. Because what may be inconvenient for us might be a blessing for someone else.

And once we recognize this and put it into practice, one of the mysteries of Sacred

Scripture begins to reveal itself. Scripture categorically states that the righteous man is safe from all of the world's calamity and suffering.

This doesn't mean that suffering is never going to affect the righteous. It means that the good man knows that God is totally in control and rests in the fact that his loving Father is going to take care of things one way or another. There can be no calamity if every single thing is ultimately in God's hands.

Ultimately, this move toward perfection, this duty of the present moment, boils down to one thing—love. Yes, faith gives us assurance and hope secures our future. But charity is the virtue that acts it all out in the right now. You don't merit salvation in the past. You don't merit salvation in the future. You merit by how you live in the right now.

Lesson Introduction

It's easy to think that once we're in the perfect will of God, everything is going to work out beautifully. Unfortunately, that's often not the case due to our fallen world. But even when abandonment to God's will gets messy, Our Lord is working for our perfection and happiness.

 **NOW BEGIN THE VIDEO**

Notes

What the Saints Say

"Those whom divine Providence is leading towards holiness in this life are tested by the following three tests: by the gift of agreeable things, such as health, beauty, fine children, money, fame and so on; by afflictions causing distress, such as the loss of children, money and fame; and by bodily sufferings, such as disease, torture and so on.

To those in the first category the Lord says, 'If a person does not forsake all that he has, he cannot be My disciple' (Luke 14:33); and to those in the second and third He says, 'You will gain possession of your souls through your patient endurance' (Luke 21:19)."

ST. MAXIMUS THE CONFESSOR — *7th Century Monk, Theologian, & Scholar*

Lectio Divina

"But before all this, they will seize you and persecute you. They will hand you over to synagogues and put you in prison, and you will be brought before kings and governors, and all on account of my name. And so you will bear testimony to me. But make up your mind not to worry beforehand how you will defend yourselves.

For I will give you words and wisdom that none of your adversaries will be able to resist or contradict. You will be betrayed even by parents, brothers and sisters, relatives and friends, and they will put some of you to death. Everyone will hate you because of me. But not a hair of your head will perish. Stand firm, and you will win life."

LUKE 21:12–18

Meditation

While most of us will never be thrown into jail and persecuted by agents of a foreign country like Fr. Walter Ciszek, every one of us will certainly face persecution of one sort or another. In fact, it may happen that even our own family will persecute us. As Christ says in Luke 21:16, "You will be betrayed even by parents, brothers and sisters, relatives and friends, and they will put some of you to death."

And in some ways, persecution by those whom we love is more difficult than even the torturous devices of foreign interrogators. This is not to diminish in any way the awful suffering of prisoners who spent time being manhandled by those who cared little for their lives. The horrors of war and captivity are brutal.

But we also know there's a special kind of pain when people are betrayed or persecuted by a member of their family. As Pope St. Gregory declared, "We are the more galled by the persecutions we suffer from those of whose dispositions we made sure, because together with the bodily pain, we are tormented by the bitter pangs of lost affection."[1]

Indeed, family-inflicted suffering cuts most deeply. The lack of love by one who should be the most affectionate increases the intensity of our agony.

This recognition should give us a new and deeper perspective on the suffering we inflict on Christ through our sin. Though we are literally his family through the sacraments, we persecute him regularly. We shrug off his loving embrace and slip the sharp knife of sin into his sacred heart.

And yet, as soon as we throw ourselves into his forgiving embrace through confession and penance, Christ immediately and lovingly welcomes us back and restores us to the family. Incredibly, he looks us in the eye and says, "not a hair on your head will perish."

So ask yourself, should we not always abandon ourselves into the hands of such a good and merciful God?

[1] Thomas Aquinas, *Catena Aurea: Commentary on the Four Gospels, Collected out of the Works of the Fathers: St. Luke*, ed. John Henry Newman, vol. 3 (Oxford: John Henry Parker, 1843), 679.

Review Questions

1. Should we expect that once we abandon ourselves to the Lord that everything will begin to work out seamlessly? Why?

2. If we rely on ourselves, are we truly abandoned to the will of God? Why?

3. The more we abandon ourselves to God, the more obscure things often become, at least for a while. To what transition in prayer does this correspond?

4. When will God finally stop teaching us to surrender and working to bring us closer to perfection? Why is this the case?

Discussion Questions

1. Even though Fr. Ciszek had already made great sacrifices and willingly put himself at great risk to preach the Gospel, he learned through terrible ordeals that he hadn't really abandoned himself to God. Have you ever had any similar experiences of learning through suffering that you were still holding part of yourself back from God even though you thought you were living according to his will? Did these experiences lead you to greater surrender? If not, has Fr. Ciszek's story given you a new perspective?

2. The more we abandon ourselves to God, the more we understand the reality that we're completely powerless without his grace. Can you think of a situation in your life in which you came to more fully realize that ultimately, God is in control and we can do nothing without him?

3. Realization of our total reliance upon grace usually happens through the difficulties and messiness of this fallen world. How have your difficult experiences and painful trials allowed you to understand this essential truth on a deeper level?

4. Reflect for a moment and ponder whether you can honestly say that when you pray for the Lord's perfect will to be done, you fully mean it. Is it really the case? Do you trust him enough to completely let go and allow him to see you through every situation and difficulty of life? Why?

Prayer Journal

LESSON SIX

Surrendering Our Memory

What We Covered in Our Last Lesson

We sometimes fall into the trap of thinking that once we're in the will of God, everything is going to work out seamlessly. Life is simply going to fall into place. But the reality is that that's rarely the case. First of all, God's will isn't "out there" somewhere. It's in the present moment. It's right now.

But also, we have to always remember that we live in a fallen world. Sin has disrupted the perfection of God's universe and it constantly presents us with bumps in the road. In fact, sometimes those bumps are more like mountains. Yet it's often in the messiness of our abandonment that God gets down to serious business.

Despite what we might like to think, our abandonment to God doesn't naturally lead to some kind of illumination whereby we see everything clearly and all becomes easy. On the contrary, the more we abandon ourselves, the more obscure things will often become, at least for a while.

This obscurity correlates to the transition from meditative to contemplative prayer. In meditation, we're focused on images, ideas and such. But as we transition into a deeper, more simplified mode of prayer in which we're content to just "be" with God—the transition into contemplation—we eventually start to experience a sensation of the lack of God's presence. We experience dryness and darkness. Even as God draws us closer, we can't feel him like we used to. And yet, the reality is that we're actually growing closer to the Lord. As we stop relying on our natural senses and feelings, he draws us more into his divine life.

It's a similar movement as we grow in true abandonment to God's will. We realize more and more that not only do we not have things figured out, but that we're powerless without the grace of God. Abandonment to God is a crushing of our self-will and fully giving ourselves over to God's will.

And most of the time, this won't happen through everything lining up perfectly, but through the difficulties and messiness presented by this fallen world. Simply put, even if we're in God's perfect will, we're imperfect people in an imperfect world. And through these imperfections God is always working to further our surrender, to further our abandonment. And he will continue to work on us until the day we stand before him for our personal judgment.

Lesson Introduction

While our abandonment to God is primarily focused upon the present, it also includes the future, as well as the past. How it relates to the future is easy to see. But how does it include the past? The answer is that every one of us has wounds from the past that can have a huge impact on our ability to grow in the spiritual life.

As we'll see in this lesson, surrendering our difficult memories to God is a vital part of our total abandonment to the Lord, which can bring about healing and transformation.

NOW BEGIN THE VIDEO

Notes

_____

_____

_____

_____

_____

_____

_____

_____

_____

_____

What the Saints Say

"We are called to pass on the healing that we have experienced, and the reconciliation that we have been given so lavishly. 'Clothe yourselves with heartfelt mercy, with kindness, humility, meekness, and patience. Bear with one another. Forgive as the Lord has forgiven you' (Colossians 3:12–13).

Having been forgiven, we are called to forgive."

POPE ST. JOHN PAUL II

Lectio Divina

"He heals the brokenhearted,

and binds up their wounds."

PSALM 147:3

Meditation

As discussed in the lesson, our ability to forgive those who have wounded us is foundational to the healing of our memory. And while this forgiveness is often extremely difficult to give, perhaps recalling the true relationship we have with each other can help.

Because while there's a definite reality to the relationship of fellow Catholics as members of the same family of God, St. Paul describes how the depth of our union is even greater than that of siblings. Yes, we are brothers and sisters in Christ. But even more, we are literally members of the same Body of Christ (Ephesians 5:30).

And this deep and mysterious relationship has a giant impact upon our need and ability to forgive one another. Indeed, in light of our status as members of the same Body, the necessity of forgiveness takes on a whole new light. How?

Well, instead of being seen as some great feat of holiness because we were able to screw up enough will power to forgive someone, once we see each other as members of the same Body, forgiveness becomes something obvious, even natural, says Fr. Wilfrid Stinissen.

In fact, he says when you think about it, "There is hardly anything to forgive. The arm does not forgive the leg because it is broken."[1] On the contrary, it strongly desires the healing of any damaged part of the body. It knows that each part is vital to the health and proper functioning of the body.

And there's a sense in which you could say this is what moves Christ so quickly to forgive us.

Even when we break communion through serious sin and damage his Mystical Body, his love heals our sin and restores us. And it's "natural" that he does so because in a real sense, he's bringing healing to his *own* body. Not in an egoistic, self-serving way, but in a self-giving way.

Never forget that our membership in his Mystical Body is pure gift. And he heals his body—he heals us—because of his infinite love.

"But what about someone who isn't part of the Body of Christ?", you might ask. "How do they fit into this since they're not part of us?"

And the answer—at least in part—is that though someone may not be in union with the Body of Christ because of sin, they were created to be a part of his Body. They have the same created destiny we do. Jesus died for them, as well. And if he offers them forgiveness, then so must we.

In fact, our membership in the Body of Christ and family of God depends upon our ability to extend forgiveness to every single person, even those opposed to us. "Love your enemies and pray for those who persecute you, so that you may be sons of your Father who is in heaven" (Matthew 5:44).

¹ *Fr. Wilfrid Stinissen, The Holy Spirit, Fire of Divine Love (San Francisco, Ignatius Press, 2017)*

Review Questions

1. Is it correct to say that forgiveness and healing are the same thing? Why?

2. Does surrender and abandonment to God mean that we may never need professional psychological assistance?

3. Where is the healing of our memories most powerfully and fully effected?

4. What are two ways we can translate the Greek word "paraclete"? How should this word bring us comfort?

5. How does trustful surrender change our negative memories into positive ones?

6. Is it necessary to "like" someone in order to forgive them?

Discussion Questions

1. We all have wounds from our past sins, relationships, and negative situations. God wants to heal all of them. What are some of the wounds you still carry from difficult past circumstances? Have you ever deliberately surrendered them to Christ?

2. In order for healing to take place, we have to be able to forgive the people who hurt us. After all, Jesus ties *our* forgiveness to our ability and desire to forgive others. (see Matthew 6:14–15) Can you think of people you have never truly forgiven? Does seeing everyone in the world as members (or potential members) of the Body of Christ help you want to forgive those who have wounded you?

3. Have you ever experienced personal healing as a result of forgiving someone else?

4. Romans 8:28 declares "that in everything God works for good with those who love him, who are called according to his purpose." How might this verse change the way you view all the bad things that have happened in your past?

Prayer Journal

_____

_____

_____

_____

_____

_____

_____

_____

_____

_____

_____

_____

LESSON SEVEN

The Difficult Surrender of Obedience

What We Covered in Our Last Lesson

We all have wounds from past sins, relationships, and negative situations, which we need to surrender to God along with everything else in our lives. If not, they can still damage us when people say or do things that dredge them up and we experience their rawness all over again.

While abandonment to God's will is necessary, it doesn't automatically heal our past wounds. Oftentimes we may need further help, and there is a legitimate place for professional psychological assistance when necessary. That said, never forget the Holy Spirit can heal us whenever he wills. We should ask him to show us the wounds of our past and give us the grace to fully accept and embrace them so as to be fully healed.

It's only once we can accept and embrace our wounds through Christ that real forgiveness and healing can take place. When we finally understand that everything that happens must go through God, we come to a deep knowledge and appreciation of the fact that even when we felt wounded, abandoned, or lost, God was always there. Even in the very midst of being wounded, he was surrounding us with his love. He was working it out so that the harm others may have intended would be transformed into grace that would save us.

And the place in which we most powerfully and fully receive that grace is in the reception of the Eucharist, what St. Ignatius of Antioch calls the "medicine of immortality." Before we approach the altar, we quote the centurion and pray, "Lord, I am not worthy to receive you, but only say the word and my soul shall be healed."

That said, healing doesn't exist in a vacuum. Our ability to fully experience the presence of God, deal with our past, and heal our memories goes hand in hand with something we often find very difficult—forgiveness. As difficult as it may be, the reality is that in order for real healing to take place, we have to be able to forgive those who wounded us. After all, Christ directly ties our forgiveness to our ability to forgive others in the Our Father.

This can be extremely hard, but God gives us the grace to do it. More specifically, he gives us the Holy Spirit, whom he calls the "Comforter," and who teaches us the truth about Christ. And the truth of Christ, in turn, purifies our memories and expels the darkness just like a candle being lit in a dark room.

This illumination and purification through the Spirit is vitally important because until our wounds are healed, our memory will be filled with all kinds of pain and disappointments, and can become the Devil's playground.

On the flipside, our memory can also serve to remind us that even difficult circumstances are a place of encounter with God. In the midst of our heartache, he was always present and sends his Spirit to draw us to himself and shifts our focus from our misery to his healing grace. In short, once we abandon our wounds and past sins to God, any negative memory we have can be transformed.

Lesson Introduction

While the word "obedience" tends to have negative connotations in modern culture, it's important to remind ourselves that obedience is a virtue. Even so, there are many layers, levels, and nuances to this topic and many things aren't quite as clear-cut as perhaps we'd like them to be.

That said, it is a topic directly connected to our ability to fully abandon ourselves to the will of the Lord that needs to be discussed.

 **NOW BEGIN THE VIDEO**

Notes

What the Saints Say

"Obedience, is rightly placed before all other sacrifices, for in offering a victim as sacrifice, one offers a life that is not one's own; but when one obeys one is immolating one's own will."

ST. GREGORY THE GREAT — *6th Century Pope & Doctor of the Church*

Lectio Divina

"But be doers of the word, and not hearers only, deceiving yourselves. For if any one is a hearer of the word and not a doer, he is like a man who observes his natural face in a mirror; for he observes himself and goes away and at once forgets what he was like.

But he who looks into the perfect law, the law of liberty, and perseveres, being no hearer that forgets but a doer that acts, he shall be blessed in his doing."

JAMES 1:22–25

Meditation

Obedience implies action. Simply knowing what God commands or what the Church teaches isn't good enough. Knowing that I should pray, for example, is far different than actually making an act of the will and doing it. Knowing that I should give alms doesn't help anybody. It's the actual act of charity that helps the poor.

In fact, James makes an interesting choice of words in the passage above.

The man who essentially glances at himself in the mirror in verse 23 quickly forgets what he looks like. But the one who "looks into the perfect law... and perseveres," is expending himself. The "look" this man gives is more than a mere glance. It is something that requires effort.

In Greek, this "look" is a "bending down", a "stooping." In fact, it's the same word used by St. Luke to describe how St. Peter stooped to look into Christ's empty tomb (see Luke 24:12). St. John uses it to describe how Mary Magdalene did the very same thing (John 20:11).

In other words, our search for the Lord can't be accomplished through passing glances. We must bend down. We must stoop. Our Lord is only found through the look of love, a love which requires obedience.

Review Questions

1. While acceptance of God's will is stage one of abandonment to our Lord, what is the second stage?

2. Why do we say that true obedience is a reflection of God himself?

3. What are some ways that God speaks to us outside of personal prayer?

4. Generally speaking, do we have a duty to obey secular authorities even when we disagree with them? Why?

Discussion Questions

1. While we don't normally think of God as exercising the virtue of obedience, the reality is that obedience is actually a reflection of God himself. The members of the Trinity offer themselves to each other in humble, obedient love. How does understanding this essential truth change your view of obedience?

2. In John 19:11, Jesus told Pilate, "You would have no power over me unless it had been given you from above." Does the fact that all authority—both secular and sacred—comes from God make you rethink your attitude toward those with legitimate authority, both inside and outside the Church? How?

3. While we have a duty to obey those in authority over us when their commands don't go against the divine law, that doesn't mean that we shouldn't work to change things we believe to be false or unholy. However, if we're going to imitate Christ, this must be done with humility and charity, which isn't always easy.

What are some ways that we can exercise these virtues when we try to change things for the better? In what way might spending time in real prayer (and perhaps even penance like fasting)—before attempting to change a bad situation—be a major help?

Prayer Journal

LESSON EIGHT

Trustful Surrender to the Church

What We Covered in Our Last Lesson

Up until now, we've been more or less focused on the initial stage of surrender, which consists of acceptance, or consent, to God's will in all circumstances. In this initial stage, we're not thrilled at the possible consequences of surrender, but will go so far as to say, "Okay, God. I'm willing."

The second stage is more active. It entails proactively doing something you know to be God's will. In other words, it's an act of obedience. And while the word "obedience" tends to have negative connotations in modern culture, it's important to remind ourselves that obedience is a virtue related to the cardinal virtue of justice.

In fact, as many saints have pointed out, obedience is directly connected to the entire notion of abandonment to God's will. And one of the reasons they say this is because true obedience is a reflection of God himself. Father, Son, and Holy Spirit are in perfect harmony with each other because they do the will of the other. They submit themselves in sacrificial, loving obedience to each other.

Of course, when we begin to talk about obedience, we're assuming that we understand exactly what we're supposed to obey. Since we're not yet in perfect harmony with God, discernment has to happen. And as always, this is where the life of prayer plays a key role. You have to be close to him in order to hear what he's telling you to do.

However, God doesn't just speak to us from within, so to speak. Discernment also comes from sources very much outside ourselves. Much of what we're supposed to obey and conform our lives to comes from the Church, which mediates God's revelation to us through Scripture, Tradition, and its teachings.

In addition to Church authorities, there are all kinds of civil authorities over us as well. Yes, they possess different levels of authority over us and only exercise it in certain areas, but their authority is very real. In fact, as Jesus declares in John 19:11, their authority comes from God himself. So we have an obligation to obey civil authorities even if they're bad people or we disagree with their decisions.

However, this doesn't mean we're required to do anything and everything both religious and secular authorities tell us. If anyone tells us to do something directly opposed to divine law, we have an obligation to disobey. We also have a right to make our opinions known with regard to things with which we disagree. And we should work to change these things we believe to be false or unholy. But whenever we exercise that right, it should always be done with the utmost charity and humility.

Lesson Introduction

We now turn directly to the issue of our obedience to the authority of the Church. And as with any discussion of authority, there are many nuances to this topic. That said, there are some general guidelines we can clearly identify, as well as serious dangers to avoid.

 **NOW BEGIN THE VIDEO**

Notes

_____

_____

_____

_____

_____

_____

_____

_____

_____

What the Saints Say

"Those whom John baptized, John baptized; those whom Judas baptized, Christ baptized.

In like manner, then, they whom a drunkard baptized, those whom a murderer baptized, those whom an adulterer baptized, if it was the baptism of Christ, were baptized by Christ. I do not fear the adulterer, the drunkard, or the murderer, because I give heed unto the dove, through whom it is said to me, 'This is He which baptizeth.'"

ST. AUGUSTINE — *4th Century Father & Doctor of the Church*

Lectio Divina

"In those days Peter stood up among the brethren (the company of persons was in all about a hundred and twenty), and said, "Brethren, the scripture had to be fulfilled, which the Holy Spirit spoke beforehand by the mouth of David, concerning Judas who was guide to those who arrested Jesus.

For he was numbered among us, and was allotted his share in this ministry.

(Now this man bought a field with the reward of his wickedness; and falling headlong he burst open in the middle and all his bowels gushed out. And it became known to all the inhabitants of Jerusalem, so that the field was called in their language Akel'dama, that is, Field of Blood.) For it is written in the book of Psalms,

'Let his habitation become desolate,

and let there be no one to live in it';

and

'His office let another take.'"

ACTS 1:15–20

Meditation

The above passage from the book of Acts is one of the clearest indications in Scripture that Church authority resides in the office and not the person. Verse twenty, "His office let another take," is a reference by St. Peter to the office held by Judas, the Disciple who betrayed Christ.

What follows in the passage is the election of Matthias to that same office. He is given apostolic authority, and this same passing on of authority has continued to this very day. (See CCC 77 & 860)

And we have to always remind ourselves that every single bishop is a "descendant" of the original Disciples due to their office. Whether or not we agree with them on a particular issue, we need to act in Christian charity towards them as persons, while maintaining the utmost respect for their office...an office given them by God.

Without turning a blind eye to sin, we need to ensure that any real or perceived sin of others does not cause us to sin ourselves.

St. John Chrysostom points out that even St. Peter, when calling out the betrayal of Judas, "does not mention him with scorn, nor say, 'that wretch,' 'that miscreant:' but simply states the fact."[1]

Think about that. Though he must have felt personally betrayed given his relationship to Judas as one of the original Twelve, Peter refuses to fall into detraction, even with regard to the one whose name is now synonymous with betrayal.

Of course, Peter doesn't leave it at that. In order to instruct those listening, he acknowledges that Judas paid the terrible price of his sin. "Falling headlong he burst open in the middle and all his bowels gushed out" (Acts 1:18).

Peter let everyone know, without any sin on his own tongue, that God's justice will ultimately be served one way or the other.

[1] John Chrysostom, "Homilies of St. John Chrysostom, Archbishop of Constantinople, on the Acts of the Apostles," in *Saint Chrysostom: Homilies on the Acts of the Apostles and the Epistle to the Romans*, ed. Philip Schaff, trans. J. Walker et al., vol. 11, A Select Library of the Nicene and Post-Nicene Fathers of the Christian Church, First Series (New York: Christian Literature Company, 1889), 18.

Review Questions

1. What are the particular areas in which bishops of the Catholic Church have authority?

2. In 1 Samuel 24, David refused to harm Saul even though Saul was trying kill him. Why? What was his reason for leaving Saul unscathed?

3. Are problems in the Church a new phenomenon?

4. What was Jesus' dire warning to those who exercise authority?

Discussion Questions

1. Padre Pio gives us a great example of humble obedience to the Church. Even though the future saint was wrongly accused and censured, he still obeyed his superiors and humbly accepted their decisions because they weren't contrary to the divine law. Why do you think he was able to act this way? What are some ways that you can imitate Padre Pio's example in your own life?

2. When we criticize Church leaders, we can easily cross the line into calumny and detraction, especially when we don't really know what's going on. What are some ways to avoid this pitfall?

3. How might meditating on the fact that the all-powerful God is perfectly aware of everything going on in the Church change the way in which we discuss and engage problems within it?

Prayer Journal

LESSON NINE

The Old Testament Obedience of Faith

What We Covered in Our Last Lesson

In our last lesson, we turned our attention to the topic of obedience to the Church and discussed one of the very important dangers we face as we deal with the issues of the day. We all know there are problems inside the Church, and navigating them is a constant struggle. Even if we're willing to obey, it's sometimes hard to know whether or not it's the right thing.

To be sure, the bishops don't have authority over every aspect of our lives. Their purview is faith and morals. Even so, regardless of whether or not we agree with them on this or that issue, they exercise a certain spiritual authority over us which we need to respect.

Also, remember nothing happens that God doesn't allow. If we are truly surrendering our lives to God, then as long as we're not being asked to break his law, like children we need to have an attitude of surrender to those in authority over us.

Never forget that God is absolutely aware of everything going on, and he's not going to simply allow people to be led astray without some kind of intervention. He loves his children far more than we do. So when we encounter problems in the Church, we need to trust that he's going to deal with them. This doesn't mean that we never say or do anything to right a wrong. There are times when we have an obligation to say or do something. However, we have to always bear in mind that God knows exactly what's going on, and we can't act as if he doesn't.

If we suspect terrible sin in the lives of those in authority over us, we should pray, offer penance, and be willing to suffer for the sake of the Body of Christ. Yes, sometimes we need to directly confront people who are committing egregious sins. That said, our natural tendency to "call people out" is often misplaced. It's extremely easy to cross the line into calumny and slander. There are few things more foolish than allowing the sins of others to lead us into sin ourselves.

Never underestimate the power of humble prayer and penance. Through it, we can offer ourselves up in sacrifice for the Church just like Jesus did. We can tap into the power of Christ crucified for both our own purification and the situation in question.

Lesson Introduction

In Hebrews chapter 11, St. Paul provides a kind of highlight reel of people who were examples of powerful obedience in the Old Testament. And when you begin to ponder the far reaching consequences of these incredible acts of faith, you begin to understand why the virtue of obedience and total surrender to God is at the very heart of spiritual progress.

NOW BEGIN THE VIDEO

Notes

What the Saints Say

"Oh! how sweet and glorious is the virtue of obedience, by which all other virtues exist, because it is the offspring of charity! On it is founded the rock of faith; it is a queen, whom he that espouses is rich in every kind of good and whom no evil can assail."

ST. CATHERINE OF SIENA — *14th Century Dominican Mystic & Doctor of the Church*

Lectio Divina

"Now faith is the assurance of things hoped for, the conviction of things not seen. For by it the men of old received divine approval. By faith we understand that the world was created by the word of God, so that what is seen was made out of things which do not appear.

By faith Abel offered to God a more acceptable sacrifice than Cain, through which he received approval as righteous, God bearing witness by accepting his gifts; he died, but through his faith he is still speaking. By faith Enoch was taken up so that he should not see death; and he was not found, because God had taken him. Now before he was taken he was attested as having pleased God. And without faith it is impossible to please him.

For whoever would draw near to God must believe that he exists and that he rewards those who seek him. By faith Noah, being warned by God concerning events as yet unseen, took heed and constructed an ark for the saving of his household; by this he condemned the world and became an heir of the righteousness which comes by faith.

By faith Abraham obeyed when he was called to go out to a place which he was to receive as an inheritance; and he went out, not knowing where he was to go. By faith he sojourned in the land of promise, as in a foreign land, living in tents with Isaac and Jacob, heirs with him of the same promise.

For he looked forward to the city which has foundations, whose builder and maker is God. By faith Sarah herself received power to conceive, even when she was past the age, since she considered him faithful who had promised. Therefore from one man, and him as good as dead, were born descendants as many as the stars of heaven and as the innumerable grains of sand by the seashore.

These all died in faith, not having received what was promised, but having seen it and greeted it from afar, and having acknowledged that they were strangers and exiles on the earth."

HEBREWS 11:1-13

Meditation

As discussed in our lesson, the story of Abraham and Isaac is identified by Scripture and Tradition as a great example of the obedience of faith. But it's more than just one more example among many. It's perhaps the most perfect Old Testament foreshadowing of the kind of obedient self-surrender God desires more than anything else. Why? Because it gets to the heart of what God has been after all along.

You see, up until Abraham's time—and for a long time thereafter—the sacrifices offered to God basically consisted of things like animals and crops. But God has never been after the blood of goats or grain.

As he declares in Isaiah 1:11, "'The multitude of your sacrifices—what are they to me?' says the Lord. 'I have more than enough of burnt offerings, of rams and the fat of fattened animals; I have no pleasure in the blood of bulls and lambs and goats.'"

Why? Because the animals, crops, and such, were merely substitutes.

What God has always wanted was the gift of ourselves, not our possessions. And while their descendants in the land of Israel greatly struggled with making this gift of self (like us), that's exactly what Abraham and Isaac offered. Both gave up the totality of their lives; the father through the gift of his own flesh embodied in his son, and the son by giving up himself.

They're perfect Old Testament examples of self-sacrificial obedience.

How fitting it is that the blood that was shed for our salvation through Christ traces its origin to the sacrifice of Abraham and Isaac. And don't forget that it's a bloodline that continues. Through the Eucharist, that same sacrificial blood now runs through our veins, as well. It gives us the power to live the virtue of obedience and totally surrender ourselves like those who have come before us.

Review Questions

1. In the book of Romans, St. Paul uses the phrase, "the obedience of faith." By this, does he mean that faith is simply an assent of the mind, or is there more to it?

2. How did Noah's obedience save him? What was he required to do?

3. What chapter of the Bible is famous for describing and praising the strong faith of many figures in salvation history?

4. What does Hebrews 11:19 tell us was the reason that Abraham was willing to go through with the sacrifice of his son?

5. Why do we say that Abraham and Isaac's obedience helped save the entire world?

6. What act of obedience did Moses and the rest of the Israelites have to perform in order to be saved from the tenth and final plague? What does this first Passover point forward to?

Discussion Questions

1. As Noah was building the ark, his neighbors were likely laughing at his apparent foolishness. They had no idea what was coming and probably thought he was crazy. In the end, though, Noah turned out to be right and his obedience proved to be well-placed.

In a very real sense, his situation isn't all that different from ours today. The modern world mocks our faith and considers us foolish. It's not unusual for a Christian to face similar contempt and ridicule that was faced by Noah. Have you ever experienced any kind of persecution or mockery for your obedience to God? If so, how did you react to it? How do you think God views us when we suffer for our faith?

2. Abraham consented to sacrifice his son Isaac even though God had already promised that his descendants would come through Isaac. This required incredible faith and trust that God would make good on his promise, no matter what. Have you ever had to exercise faith in God in a seemingly impossible situation? How did God carry you through the trial? Did the situation and it's result bring you closer to God?

Prayer Journal

_____

_____

_____

_____

_____

_____

_____

_____

_____

_____

_____

_____

_____

LESSON TEN

Total Surrender Through Christ

What We Covered in Our Last Lesson

Our faith in God and growth in surrender should lead to action, an action that saves us. St. Paul spells all of this out in the book of Romans. In fact, he uses a particular phrase—"the obedience of faith"—in the very beginning and at the very end of the book (Romans 1:5 and 16:26).

And this is a curious phrase because we tend to think of faith simply as an assent of the mind. However, Paul ties faith not just to mental assent, but to action. For him, faith isn't just believing. It's a total, active surrender to God's will. And it saves us because it demonstrates that surrender.

We can see this same active, faithful obedience greatly praised in another place in Scripture: Hebrews chapter 11. This passage lists members of a kind of ancient faith "hall of fame" and describes how strong faith led these figures to fully surrender to God in obedience, an obedience that saved them.

For example, it mentions Noah and his famous Ark. In this familiar story, we learn that sin had gotten so bad following Adam's fall that God decided to start over. So he told Noah to build a giant boat that would house his family and all the animals God wanted to save. And even though his neighbors were probably laughing in his face, Noah's radical obedience saved him from the coming flood.

Hebrews 11 also references the incredible faith of Abraham and his son Isaac. Back in the book of Genesis, God asked Abraham to do the unthinkable, to sacrifice his only son after he'd waited 100 years to receive him. Incredibly, Abraham obeyed. What's more, Isaac also consented to his sacrifice. He willingly offered himself in sacrifice, according to his father's wishes. And through the obedient faith of both Abraham and Isaac, the entire world was saved. God spared Isaac and promised to bless the world through Abraham. This promise was fulfilled through Jesus Christ, who was descended from Abraham and Isaac's line.

Likewise, Hebrews 11 also mentions the first Passover. In the book of Exodus, we read of the famous 10 plagues, the tenth one being the most harrowing. The Angel of Death was going to kill all the firstborns in the land. In order to avoid this plague, the Israelites had to kill an unblemished male lamb, spread its blood on the doorpost, and eat it. When the Angel of Death saw the sacrificial blood marked on the lintel of the door, he would "pass over" that house and leave its firstborn unharmed. It was through this active obedience that the Israelites were saved.

Lesson Introduction

While the Cross of Christ is the foundation upon which our faith is built, St. Maximus the Confessor tells us there's an earlier event in the Passion of Our Lord that plays an absolutely vital role. In fact, this pivotal scene was just as much a requirement for our salvation as the Cross itself. And it's a scene that needs to play out in each of our lives in order for us to be united to the Lord and be saved.

 **NOW BEGIN THE VIDEO**

Notes

What the Saints Say

"Naturally we all have an inclination to command, and a great aversion to obey; and yet it is certain that it is more for our good to obey than to command; hence perfect souls have always had a great affection for obedience, and have found all their joy and comfort in it."

ST. FRANCIS DE SALES — *17th Century Doctor of the Church & Author of* Introduction to the Devout Life

Lectio Divina

"Not every one who says to me, 'Lord, Lord,' shall enter the kingdom of heaven, but he who does the will of my Father who is in heaven. On that day many will say to me, 'Lord, Lord, did we not prophesy in your name, and cast out demons in your name, and do many mighty works in your name?' And then will I declare to them, 'I never knew you; depart from me, you evildoers.'"

MATTHEW 7:21–23

Meditation

Trustful surrender cannot be dissociated from humble obedience. They are blood brothers. In fact, without true obedience we're not getting into heaven. That's why Christ says in Matthew 7, that "Not every one who says to me, 'Lord, Lord,' shall enter the kingdom of heaven, but he who does the will of my Father who is in heaven" (v. 7).

We can only truly come to know Christ by doing his will through obedient surrender. Why? Because it's how we are joined to him. Through obedience our will becomes one with his and we are unified with him.

And if this doesn't happen, we aren't truly in relationship with him. We're strangers whom he won't recognize when we stand before him at our personal judgment. He doesn't know us because he doesn't see himself reflected in us.

And while it might seem unmerciful to some that Jesus is ordering people to depart from him, don't forget that love without justice isn't really love. If a man says he loves his wife, but repeatedly cheats on her, is that love? Obviously not. There is no real union of persons.

And the same is true in our relationship with Christ.

If we repeatedly cheat on and abuse our Bridegroom Messiah through disobedience, do we really love him? If we continually refuse to unify ourselves with his humble gift of self, do we really know him? Of course not. So how can we expect him to receive us with open arms at the threshold of heaven?

Review Questions

1. Jesus' crucifixion was the climax of his Passion. What particular moment shortly before Christ went to the Cross does St. Maximus the Confessor say was the catalyst for the entire event?

2. If Jesus is God, how did he increase in "wisdom and stature," as indicated in the Gospel of Luke?

3. How does the book of Hebrews say that Jesus learned obedience? In other words, what specific thing did he experience in his humanity that led to this learning?

4. Why does our obedience save us? More to the point, what is it about our relationship to Christ that empowers our obedience to save us?

5. When Jesus surrendered himself to the Father in his Passion and death, he was obedient in our stead. His obedience was on behalf of all humanity. Does this mean that he got us off the hook so we no longer have to be obedient to legitimate authority?

Discussion Questions

1. The final stage of abandonment to God is being his instrument and letting him use you in whatever way he wills. Are there areas in your life which are a great struggle to completely surrender to God? What fears are holding you back from doing so? Can you identify areas in which you've already surrendered and God is using you as an instrument of salvation?

2. When Jesus prayed in Gethsemane, he asked the Father to rescue him from his upcoming Passion and death. But at the end of his prayer, he humbly and obediently submitted to the Father's will and accepted the Father's plan for him.

Have you ever specifically prayed that the Lord would help you completely surrender so that he can use you for the salvation of the world? In light of this series, is offering yourself in complete surrender something for which you will strive? If so, what are some practical things you will do in order to make it happen?

Prayer Journal

Summary of Lesson Ten

This lesson marked our transition into the third stage of abandonment, which is being God's instrument. Being God's instrument means we surrender ourselves to the point where the Lord can use us in whatever way he wills. Beyond just accepting or doing his will, it's a movement *into* God's will. This movement saves and deifies us because it joins us to Christ's obedience.

The truth of this comes to light in the book of Hebrews where we learn that Jesus "learned obedience through what he suffered" (Hebrews 5:8). This passage is referencing Jesus' agony in the garden when he sweat blood in Gethsemane. And this difficult moment of obedience is the pivotal moment in Christ's Passion.

Yes, the crucifixion is the climax, but without Gethsemane the crucifixion doesn't happen. In fact, St. Maximus the Confessor says the battle was won even before the Cross because it was in Gethsemane that Jesus surrendered his will. That was the key moment: "Not my will, but thine, be done." It was total victory through total surrender.

And his act of the will, his "yes," gave us all the ability to tap into his obedience through our own obedient "yes." Our obedience grafts us into the vine of Christ. Since we are a part of his Mystical Body, it actually takes hold of and penetrates Christ's obedience. Put simply, we are saved through our obedience united to the obedience of Christ.

Yes, it can sometimes be extremely hard. Yes, it will grate on our humanity. But isn't that the point? We don't want to stay only human. We want to become divine through the grace of Jesus Christ. And obedience—trustful and total surrender to God—is the key.

Take the next step!

Go to ScienceOfSainthood.com today and experience a whole new level of prayer and relationship with God!

"Blown away"

"I can hardly believe how wonderful this is."

Courses in the Science of Sainthood include:

Introduction to Real Prayer

The 7 Deadly Sins

The Moral Virtues

The Theological Virtues

The Dark Night of the Soul

Total Abandonment to God's Will

St. Teresa of Avila's 9 Grades of Prayer

The Gifts of the Spirt ...and more!

"If you've ever wanted to deepen your life of prayer and actually make some progress in avoiding vice and growing in virtue, then look no further. The Science of Sainthood is for you."

–Dr. Brant Pitre, *Renowned theologian & author of* Jesus and the Jewish Roots of the Eucharist

ScienceofSainthood.com

Scan the QR Code with your Phone's Camera & Tap the Link!

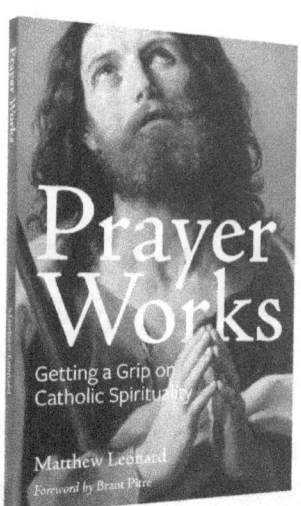